Self-Help Books Don't Work: But This One Will

A Memoir

Dr. Laura Williamson

BALBOA.PRESS

A DIVISION OF HAY HOUSE

Balboa Press books may be ordered through booksellers or by contacting:

Balboa Press
A Division of Hay House
1663 Liberty Drive
Bloomington, IN 47403
www.balboapress.com
1 (877) 407-4847

Because of the dynamic nature of the Internet, any web addresses or links contained in this book may have changed since publication and may no longer be valid. The views expressed in this work are solely those of the author and do not necessarily reflect the views of the publisher, and the publisher hereby disclaims any responsibility for them.

The author of this book does not dispense medical advice or prescribe the use of any technique as a form of treatment for physical, emotional, or medical problems without the advice of a physician, either directly or indirectly. The intent of the author is only to offer information of a general nature to help you in your quest for emotional and spiritual well-being. In the event you use any of the information in this book for yourself, which is your constitutional right, the author and the publisher assume no responsibility for your actions.

Any people depicted in stock imagery provided by Getty Images are models, and such images are being used for illustrative purposes only. Certain stock imagery © Getty Images.

Print information available on the last page.

ISBN: 978-1-9822-4654-9 (sc)
ISBN: 978-1-9822-4655-6 (e)

Balboa Press rev. date: 04/21/2020

Dedication

To those who are about to give up on themselves as ever being able to change, this book is for you. This book is for the diehards. Those people who drive to an ex's house and wonder how they got there (again), who answer a phone call from a toxic friend, knowing they'll get sucked in to their drama (yet again), and those who can't stop eating chips until the bag is gone (one more time). I got you. There is a way out of these seemingly hopeless situations and a way to have the life that you *really* want.

This book is dedicated to you!

Contents

Introduction ix

Chapter 1   Why Self-Help Books Don't Work: 1

Chapter 2   More Reasons Why They Don't Work:

               Inability to Land 19

Chapter 3   Drivers, Start Your Neurons! 27

Chapter 4   One Final Suggestion: 41

Chapter 5   Your Turn 51

A Note to Writers of Self-Help Books 59

Additional Resources 61

References 67

Acknowledgements 71

About the Author 75

Introduction

"That which seems most feeble and bewildered

in you is the strongest and most determined"

Kahlil Gibran "The Prophet" (p. 92)

"Right is a cage, not a freedom"

Bill P, Todd W, Sara S "Drop the Rock" (p. 50)

You're like me, I know. You've read all the books, gone to the workshops on breathing, meditation, yoga, "The Work" by Byron Katie, Est, Landmark, been to therapy, even become a therapist, etc. and still you do not have the life that you want. Sound familiar? Yep, been there.

Why do you and I still not have the life that we want? There is one last stumbling block for people like us. It isn't that we aren't smart or successful in our careers, it's that we still find ourselves looking at our lives from the outside, as if we're a character in a movie or book, and still unsatisfied and unhappy. We just can't quite cross that finish line. That was me for years and years. However, thanks to the strategies that I have covered in this book, I was finally able to put all the pieces together, started feeling like a whole and well person and wanted to share how I did it with you fine folks. I am finally living the life that I want and have never been happier!

Can't wait and want to know how I did it right now? Here's a teaser, we can't have the life that we want because all the self-help books, classes, retreats, etc. are assuming a false baseline. They assume that our minds are working properly, and they aren't. The material presented in these books, retreats, online courses, etc. is also presented in a way that will not get through (at least to many of us). We are just plainly unable to take in and apply what all those well-meaning people, books and classes suggest, because our minds are so &^%$-d up and the material is bewildering. In order to take in and effectively apply all this "self-help" literature, the baseline needs to be fixed (or healed) and the material needs to be reorganized with us in mind.

Why? In order to incorporate suggestions from these well-meaning authors, each idea must be learned in conjunction with the others, because in isolation, they make no sense. To know how to, "let something go," (for example), a person must understand each of the components that come together to create that particular "letting go" skill such as seeing their own boundaries, having an internal locus of control, recognizing other, having a well-connected and functioning mind, etc. This is called, high element interactivity. The idea is that the interaction between each aspect is essential to understanding how to incorporate the overall idea (such as letting go). Here's the problem with that, material with high element interactivity requires a higher resource or "load" of cognition. In English, that means that things that are hard to learn, such as "create the life that I want," will be even harder because it is complex and therefore requires more brain power (aka cognitive load). What we will see is that we are trying to incorporate these changes in our lives with a broken projector (the mind), using material that the mind doesn't understand. This may sound depressing, and it can be if you don't take the actions suggested in this book, but if you do, rest assured that it works.

I'm going to show you how to un-^%$ your mind once and for all, apply the concepts from these books, and get going on that life that you want. An awesome, rich, full, life is not only for the Gwyneth Paltrow's of the world. It's for you too! You deserve it. Ready? Let's go!

Chapter 1

Why Self-Help Books Don't Work:
(aka How the mind gets %$#^!)

"Nothing can come into our experience unless it finds something in us with which is it attuned"

Emmet Fox "Sermon on the Mount" (p. 45)

We may not think so, but most everyone (if not everyone) thinks that they "know" reality. Just ask any person a simple question like, "how's it going?" and they'll respond with a narrative about their life. Meaning, how their particular life is going, from their own specific perspective. Now, if you notice that one or two of the thoughts that they share are not true, or perhaps slightly off, you can push against it, and maybe come out of the conversation unscathed, and maybe not. Turns out that people aren't keen on holes being poked in their sense of reality. Let's take an example from my own life. I remember starting to "date" a man that I met in a 12-step program. He shared with me that he wasn't working, that he had a girlfriend, but "it wasn't going well," and that his first girlfriend was a prostitute. I remember thinking, "wow, that's weird," but I didn't think it meant anything about him, or her for that matter, and maybe it didn't. Of course, I told my friends all about this new wonderful guy and they didn't share my enthusiasm for him. The pointed out that having a ton of free time, being super "friendly" with people (especially new women) in our program, that he was throwing his current girlfriend "under the bus," were actually inconsistent with his "great share" in our meetings. I couldn't see it. In fact, they said things like, "Laura, maybe he's not right for you," and "maybe his behavior is a "red flag" and not a work around," and "maybe you should focus on your own life," which was not at all how I saw things at the time or had any interest in doing. Did I listen to my friends, you ask? No, I kept seeing him.

Looking back on it what I was doing was avoiding responsibility for myself by attaching to a person who was emotionally unavailable. I also assigned magical qualities to him. He had such a great share and seemed so well, given how "popular" he was in our 12-step home group, that I idealized and pursued him, then blamed him for not fulfilling my fantasies and expectations. I really had no idea who he was, or it turns out who I was, so because I had such few healthy boundaries, I became sexually involved with and emotionally attached without knowing him. To say it was a dark time, only touches the tip of the emotional iceberg. I frequently found myself on the floor of my bedroom or bathroom, curled up in the fetal position, crying myself to sleep. I tried to hold it together in front of my two-daughters, but honestly could see no way out of the situation. I thought I had ruined my life and it was just getting worse. Keep in mind that at this time, I had already spent $1,000's on talk-therapy, had three academic degrees, was very successful professionally, and was sober several years. Aren't I supposed to be well by now? I'd read the books, followed the steps, took the suggestions, but still fell short of the well mark. Talk about hopeless!

The good news is that this very painful and dark path, eventually landed me here with you writing this book. So, the reason I kept seeing him, and behaved in a manner that was so contrary to what I wanted follows. The simple answer is that I could not hear my friends, or therapists, or understand the well-meaning self-help book authors, or process what they were saying, and therefore could not stop the behavior. The reasons and solutions are the basis of this book, which I am writing because if I could help anyone sidestep that level of despair by sharing my story and how I got out, I would. Here goes.

To begin to understand what happened with me, it's important to hear my background. I was born in the late 60's, the youngest of three kids, to a single mother. Well, she wasn't single, but if you hear the stories, she might as well have been. I had heard over and over, from everyone on that side of the family, about my miserable father, what a drunk and philanderer he was, how much everything cost, how hard it was, etc. I'm sure it was, certainly sounded like it!

Of course, I had no idea what any of that really meant, other than it was a real drag for everyone involved. I was just living my life. I had two older brothers, that were (as you can imagine) typical annoying boys. They bothered me almost continually with teasing and fighting, some of which I'm sure I started and some of which was a product of our times, and still others a result of our home life. Here, let me give you a morsel of their thoughtfulness.

I remember Michael, the one 2-years older than me, "accidentally" killing my hamster Ebenezer when I was around nine and my older brother David asking, "do you have pubic hair yet?" when I was around twelve. Really!?! Unbelievable! What jerks! This was not unusual in our home. It was the late 60s and throughout the 70s remember, so (for those of you who were around, you know) it was a party, just not for the kids. What this looks like to a child is that lots of people were in the house that we didn't know. They were having a good time, and some thought it would be cute to get the kids stoned. That last part is courtesy of my brother's memory, because I don't recall getting stoned as a child. I do remember drinking. There was always booze in the house, is what I remember. My first drunk was drinking my stepfather's frozen gin, one night when I had a pile of girls sleeping over at my house. The second or third drunk found me "coming to" out on the Palouse Highway South of Spokane, Washington. Now, we lived in Spokane at the time, so the location wasn't a stretch, but the behavior was telling. What I remember about that moment was the sharpness of the rocks under my feet as a problem when I started to walk. Apparently I had lost my shoes. This is what they call foreshadowing, people. Over the years, I would regularly "come to" without shoes. Also, you might wonder where my parents were and how did I get there. No idea!

Anyway, as younger children we lived with our mother in Hawaii and Northern California most of the year and went to stay with our father in Bakersfield, California for summers. What is truer, is that we stayed with our grandparents in Westminster, California over the summers and "visited" our father periodically. This was perfectly fine with me by-the-way because my father was a drunk (as previously indicated). Well, can someone be considered a drunk, if they have a job? This guy seemed to be able to keep his job, so maybe not, and who am I to diagnose? Either way, one of my fondest memories was being left in his pick-up truck with my brothers, while he was in the bar, drinking. Nice. That may have been an indicator. The other, perhaps larger indicator was his lack of interest in parenting or in us as kids. How could I tell, you ask? Well, he wasn't around, didn't call, didn't send birthday cards, etc. That'll do it.

Right around the time of the "coming to" on the highway incident, my oldest brother had just been killed. This was the final nail in the coffin for me as an adolescent trying to have a "normal" life. I was 15 and he was 18. David was what one known to be "troubled." He was brilliant in my estimation, always got the best grades, read those mammoth sized (Lord of the Rings) type books, and was fun to hang out with. David was my soul. I looked up to him, followed him around, wanted to be with him or at least near him. Once he started reading, I knew it would be hours and I would wait for him to take a break in hopes that we could go outside and play handball at the park or go swimming together. I'm sure that irritated him and of course, we would fight. He spent time in juvenile delinquency detention center and lived in what we now call "sober living," but I think it was a boy's farm of some sort. My other brother, Michael, followed suit mostly. All of us struggled with getting and staying sober. David had just gotten sober prior to being killed by a drunk driver. He was riding his bike near the sober living facility and was hit. I remember the call coming into our house in Spokane because my mother screamed. She cried and held me while she rocked on the edge of her bed.

I officially checked-out at this point. That was it. It was a Saturday and I went to my track meet. "Just another day in my life" was the thought that I had. You would not be able to connect with me again for nearly thirty years.

So, all these experiences are what medical and counseling professionals call trauma. I was plainly traumatized as a child and (to get back to the point of this book) because of that the baseline (that is my functioning mind), was off kilter. Newer trauma research is showing that a person doesn't have to go through a major traumatic event, such as plane crash or experience severe child abuse to be considered traumatized. We now understand that there are smaller-sized traumas, that likely affect every person in the world. For example, a child whose reality was not acknowledged as "real" by a care giver, is now considered traumatized. Understanding that trauma dramatically affects the way that our minds function is critical to understanding why all these self-help books aren't working. We simply are unable to process information and learn the way other people do. That's it! It's simple, but not easy, my friends. You and I are going to walk together down some dark paths but know that this is the way out and the way to freedom. Adding this piece to the puzzle will allow you to create the life that you want. Believe me when I say that I know.

Here is the second important aspect of trauma for those of us wanting to "get" something from all these self-help books and well-meaning classes, to consider. Why are traumatized people not able to process information the way that "normal" people do? Here's the problem. So, as luck would have it, I studied cognition in my doctoral program. I know, right? So great! In my dissertation (Williamson, 2004), I specifically looked at Richard E. Mayer's cognitive theory of multimedia learning (1996, 1997, 2001), which suggests that meaningful learning occurs when the person engages in three basic kinds of cognitive processes: selecting, organizing, and integrating. Sorry to be so academic, but I figured you were like me, and would prefer to know what the &^%$ is going on here! Bear with me, it will make sense as we move forward.

So, selecting involves paying attention to relevant aspects of the presented material (such as hot guys on some reality TV show), organizing involves constructing a coherent structure (such as hot guy sees other hot person of interest and they "fall in love" on said reality TV show), and integrating involves building connections with existing knowledge (such as relating "falling in love" on TV to my concrete experiences in my non TV relationships).

Mayer's basic hypothesis is that people seek to make sense of the world by building coherent mental representations. He bases this hypothesis on the human information processing system, which he describes in his theory as diagrammed in Figure 1.

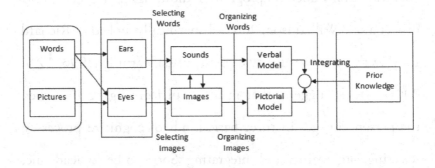

Figure 1. Cognitive Theory of Multimedia Learning

Mayer (2001) goes on to state that humans process information in what he terms the presentation modes view of learning. The presentation modes view proposes that learners are able to use various cognitive coding systems to represent knowledge, such as verbal and pictorial knowledge representations. This theory is consistent with Paivio's dual-coding theory (Paivio, 1986, 1991; Clark & Paivio, 1991; Sadoski & Paivio, 2001; Mayer & Sims, 1994), which assumes that individuals have separate processing channels for verbal and pictorial knowledge.

"The reason I made friends with the wind –

with reality – is that I discovered I didn't have

a choice. I realized that it's insane to oppose

it. When I argue with reality, I lose – but only

100 percent of the time. How do I know that

the wind should blow? It's blowing."

Byron Katie "Loving What Is" (p. 2)

A little more academic talk, please...we're getting there. According to Anderson (1973), a schema (singular) represents generic knowledge. A general category (schema) will include slots for all the components, or features, included in it. Schemata (plural) are embedded one within another at different levels of abstraction. Relationships among them are conceived to be like webs (rather than hierarchical); thus, each one is interconnected with many others.

This web aspect of schema is critical to understanding our minds and therefore our lives. To give you another way to understand this point, consider the difference between linear and non-linear thinking. Linear thinking is typically characterized as a step-by-step process, where there is sequential order, clear delineations and parameters between variables. When we think of a straight line, for example, we think it is the best way to get from one place to another because it is the shortest distance! Linear thinkers pride themselves on their precision, they are cut and dry, black and white, no in-between people. They think they are compromising and come to quick resolutions, but what is truer is that they can't see beyond their own limited scope and as a result, their solutions only scratch the surface.

Non-linearity folks, on the other hand, recognize that there is no such thing as linearity. They see that all things as existing within a web. Minds, people, problems, variables, or whatever word you want to use as a starting point, all extend in a myriad of directions and then come back again. So, if relationships between variables exist within a web, then we have to traverse multiple directions in order to see (let alone solve) our life problems.

For example, years ago I hired someone to help me devise a faculty evaluation process at my university. I had the tool, I needed help creating a process and then rolling it out to the school. The person I hired, didn't have an extensive background in higher education, nor was a faculty member, so his suggestions lacked depth. When confronted with a specific faculty instructional issue, I remember his response was, "this instructor needs time-management training?' That is an example of linear thinking. It was understandable, but only sought to solve a surface symptom. What I needed and would search for was the central root and causation, which revealed a web of instructional and curriculum variables to consider.

So, back to the issue at hand, how do we support people to attend to schema acquisition (aka learn new things, or stop destructive patterns)? As I mentioned, cognitive load theory has some suggestions (Sweller & Chandler, 1994; Sweller & Chandler, 1991). The theory notes that schema acquisition is the building block of behavior and may be summarized as follows: (a) Schema acquisition requires attention directed to problem states and their associated moves; other cognitive activities must remain limited and peripheral so as not to impose a heavy cognitive load that interferes with learning. (b) Encouraging or requiring people to engage in means-ends search or to integrate multiple sources of information misdirects attention and imposes a heavy cognitive load. (c) Because integrating multiple sources of information misdirects attention and imposes a heavy cognitive load, schema acquisition cannot commence until disparate sources of information have been mentally integrated. (d) Material with reduced or unitary sources of information will reduce or eliminate the need for people to use cognitive resources to restructure material into a form suitable for schema acquisition. (e) Learning is enhanced when people are allowed to attend to schema acquisition rather than to information reformulation, which is the case with learning new things. Got it?

In know it's a lot, so if you want to skip ahead, I get it. Just know that it's here and you can come back for more information as you need it. For those of you staying, one more point about cognition and conditions of the mind. Beyond schema acquisition, Sweller and Chandler (1994) reveal two important points to deconstruct with respect to the strategy of integrating: the material and the method of delivery. To illustrate their point about the material, the authors provide an example.

A student learning elementary algebra must learn how to multiply out the denominator of one side of an equation in order to isolate a single pronumeral in the numerator on that side. The student needs to learn what to do when faced with an equation such as a/b = c, solve for a. To learn this process, the student must learn that, when multiplying by b, the numerator on the left-hand side is multiplied by b, giving ab; the two bs on the left-hand side cancel out, leaving a isolated; because the left-hand side has been multiplied by b, the right-hand side must also be multiplied by b; multiplying the right-hand side by b gives cb in the numerator on the right-hand side; the denominator remains unchanged at 1, which is not shown in the equation; the net consequence is a = cb, which meets the goal of isolating the numerator on the left-hand side of the equation. (p. 189)

Each step in the algebra equation must be learned in conjunction with the others, because in isolation, they do not make mathematical sense. This goes back to our non-linearity thinking ideas. To know how to multiply out a denominator, you must understand how to perform the other operations. The authors call this feature of the material high element interactivity. I mentioned that in the introduction. The suggestion is that the interaction between each step is essential to understanding the equation. Material with high element interactivity requires a higher resource or "load" of cognition. Sweller and Chandler note that "complexes of elements that are irreducibly large because they consist of many connecting elements may tax our limited processing capacity and so impose a heavy cognitive load" (p. 189).

The implementation of specific strategies designed to engage us in three basic kinds of cognitive processes: selecting, organizing, and integrating and to attend to schema acquisition can positively affect our ability to learn new behaviors.

> **"Yesterday I was clever, so I wanted to change the world. Today I am wise, so I am changing myself."**
>
> **— Rumi**

The good and the bad news

Why does this matter? For those of us trying to change our lives, understanding that our minds as well as the material are off kilter, is essential. To that end, I've got some good new and some bad news. Which would you like first? The bad? Okay, here it is, as you have read, the mind has a mind of its own. It does its own thing. If you think that you're in charge, you're not. Of the 50,000 thoughts you had yesterday, guess how many you will have again today? Almost 50,000. Yes, the mind repeats itself and repeats itself. If you learned something when you were a child, no matter how much you want to change that thought or the associated behavior, you have not been able to do so, I get you. If you want to stop thinking about that girl or boy or they, or stop eating that entire pizza, I have news for you. It won't be easy because it won't be easy to change your behavior, because it won't be easy to change your mind.

What the good news? It's not only possible, but entirely within your reach to change your mind and therefore your life. It's going to require some dedication and focus, but if I can do it, and I have, then you can do it, and I'm going to tell you how. Keeping reading, you got this!

Chapter 2

More Reasons Why They Don't Work: Inability to Land

> "Perception is impossible without a belief in "more" or "less." At every level it involves selectivity."
>
> A Course in Miracles (p. 41).

From the moment I can recall a thought, I remember wondering, "what the %^$& this was all about?" I had a gazillion questions and no answers. I distinctly recall looking around the room as a child and wondering, "Who were these people" and "what the &$^% is going on around here?"

What else was going on, you ask? Well, I shared some of it in a previous chapter, but what I need to add now is around cultural influences on the mind. If you remember, my childhood occurred during the late 60s and throughout the 70s. When I consider my life, I think of what Jurgen Habermas (1981) calls a lifeworld. Yes, I was a philosophy major, so prepare yourself for that also! Anyway, Habermas makes the point that each person has a lifeworld and that each of us can never fully step outside of our own lifeworld, meaning we always see life from our particular perspective and it's not possible to see it (at least fully) from the perspective of another. My lifeworld was influenced by the 60s in Southern California, where I was born, and Hawaii and Northern California in the 70s, where I was raised. If I look back at the late 60's, I think of the Vietnam War, the assassinations of Martin Luther King Jr, Malcolm X, Bobby and Jack Kennedy, and the gay and civil rights movement. From what I have been told and seen on Netflix, the 60s and 70s were a time of great unrest in the world, or what I would today call trauma, in the country. Have you seen the Ken Burns documentary, "the Vietnam War?" I rest my case. As a child, I remember the yellow ribbons tied on trees for soldiers missing in action, the protests, and of course the war, all of which have contributed to my experience of my world.

"The answers to these questions provided me with knowledge about my reactions to the conditions in my life"

The Big Book of Alcoholics Anonymous (p. 468)

So, let's circle back and discuss Mayer's strategies for learning new stuff. Here's the tough part, if you grew up in and around any type or trauma, your ability to select, organize, and integrate the "right" information and therefore attend to schema acquisition (aka to make good or health choices for yourself) are nil. This is where we begin this chapter. I want to add one more layer to the challenge you are facing and that is around cultural trauma. I shared above some of the cultural trauma from my childhood, but let's talk about current trauma of 2020. Just a month ago, Seattle (where I live) became the epicenter of the global coronavirus pandemic. The entire city is shut down as I write this chapter. Schools are closed, store shelves are empty, and everyone is practicing social distancing. Keep in mind that this isn't the only event traumatizing us right now. We also have the economic slowdown, job loss, children in cages at the Southern US border, a President continually tweeting his irrational directives and on and on. We're collectively facing uncertainty as a people. The effective this has on us as a people and individually is called lack of differentiation of self and multigenerational emotional processing, both of which (on top of everything else we have covered) dramatically affect our ability to create the life that we want.

> **"Differentiation of self is the capacity to think and reflect, to not respond automatically to emotional pressures. Undifferentiated people are easily moved to emotionality. Their lives are ruled by reactivity to those around them"**
>
> **- Michael Nichols (p. 79).**

Okay, I guess I caught undifferentiation as a child. It must be contagious. I do remember getting chicken pox as a freshman in high school, but do not remember catching this, but that quote above describes my family interaction to a "T" and describes life today on social media and in face-to-face interactions also to a "T." I see people all around me who do not possess self-restraint or differentiation when it comes to difficult topics. From co-workers to Facebook friends, to strangers, people seem to lack the ability to maintain a balance emotionally or in their thinking when it comes to current events. Case in point, after the coronavirus hit, there was a run on toilet paper in the grocery stores. There is none left (at the time of this writing) at my local store. What does toilet paper have to do with the virus? The only connection is in the mind of the traumatized people in my city. There is a definite lack of differentiation.

"Something is at work mending the cut on my hand right now, as if hidden in the skin with atomic knitting needles"

Anne Lamont "Hallelujah Anyway: Rediscovering Mercy" (p. 125-6).

Another emotional virus picked up culturally is what's called, "multigenerational emotional processes." I know that sounds made up, but it's a thing. I see it all around me (again at work, on Facebook, and with strangers). It is basically the interconnected patterns of undifferentiated emotions. What is that, you ask? Well, it has to do with enmeshment. What this looks like is, you feel how I feel, and think how I think, and do how I do. Our friend Michael Nichols (2013) says that, "Lack of differentiation in a family produces emotionally reactive children, which may be manifest as emotional over-involvement or emotional cutoff from the parents, which in turn leads to fusion in new relationships— because people with limited emotional resources tend to project all their needs onto each other" (p. 79). Sound familiar? Remember mom as single parent and dad as, checked-out? Neither of my parents had any sense of how to care for their own needs nor as a result were able to teach those skills to me or my brothers.

If any of you had similar experiences you know your internal voice and how critical it sounds. It's like a simmering pot of water of negative thoughts, on all the time, and pestering you with, "you're not enough," you're unworthy of love," "you'll never measure up," "why bother," "no one cares," and on and on. You know the list. You have the list. After reading this book so far, you know now that having this internal voice, means that we are unwittingly attracting to ourselves those with the same mental attunement. For mates, bosses, etc. we get those who perpetuate the cycle. We certainly don't mean to and would love for it to stop! All forms of trauma affect us, and as a result, our self-image and our relationships with the world and with others. If our internal processes are not functioning as they were intended, we experience physical, emotional, and behavioral problems.

An example of this is what I call the "spin up." I have a coworker who anytime he has a thought, not only must share it, but he will not stop talking until all of us, whomever is in the room, hears his full story. If he gets interrupted, he waits until the room is quiet again, and starts talking (on his own topic) until interrupted once more. Keep in mind that it doesn't matter if the story is appropriate (or connected in any way) to the topic of the meeting. He is completely self-obsessed. He puts an unusual amount of energy into the particular issue of the day. He then creates elaborate illusions (or what to the rest of us sound like fantasy) around the issue. He is completely invested in his illusion of the day, at all times. From the outside, he looks like he is unwilling to "let go," of whatever the issue is, but what is more true is that he is unable to let go. The more energy he devotes to his illusion, the more he has invested in it being true, the less he is able to see the fallacy of his ways, nor have any real understanding. He seems to live his life in a "spun up" state. When I hear him, all I can think is that he must have been traumatized. His mind is completely disconnected from the reality that the rest of us share. But you know that already. You probably know people like that, and/or have been that person yourself.

Parents, bosses, coworkers, and friends do what I suspect yours did too, they can't help themselves. They project their needs and emotional conflicts onto others, you and me. I ended up marrying a man who came from the same family dynamic, which produced emotional distance and emotional dysfunction within our marriage, which of course we passed right onto our daughters.

Sorry to end on a depressing note. It really is darkest before the dawn. It gets WAY better from here. Hold tight for the ride, friends. The solution is in the next chapter. Let's go!

Chapter 3

Drivers, Start Your Neurons!

> "Even if the voice is relevant to the situation at hand, it will interpret it in terms of the past. This is because the voice belongs to your conditioned mind, which is the result of all your past history as well as the collective cultural mind-set you inherited"
>
> **Eckhart Tolle "The Power of Now" (p. 18)**

Here we are finally! Thanks for your patience. I wanted to make sure you knew what was happening in your mind and what you were up against. Keep in mind that, just as bad as the situation may appear, please know that the solution is equally amazing and effective.

The first part of the solution has to do with neuroscience. I know it sounds crazy, but it's true, so bear with me. Remember that guy with all the free time and the prostitute girlfriend that I started dating back in chapter one? Turns out that he and I had a lot in common. Of course, I didn't see it that way for years. I thought for sure, he was the one with the problem, not me. Well, here's the problem, in order for me to even be attracted to someone like that, I had to have something inside of me that was attuning at that same level, or wavelength, or turns out, similar neural functioning. Yes, the neurology of my mind was messing with me and needed to be addressed first.

I shared with you all about my earlier childhood, cultural, and current societal traumas. Now, let me take a second to acknowledge that there are many who have more significant childhood, cultural, and societal traumas in their lives than me and might be reading my story saying, "please girl!" I am here to tell you that the mind doesn't care. It doesn't distinguish between BIG trauma and small trauma; it sees it all the same.

Also, I acknowledge that even though we may have shared societal and cultural traumas, that we all experienced together, that some of you actually were in the Vietnam (or other) War, some of you were jailed for your beliefs and/or physically abused, so please know that I am not saying our experiences were the same. I am sorry you had that experience. I really am. It sucks completely. All I am saying is that the mind doesn't distinguish neurologically.

Back to the guy with the prostitute and extra time for a moment. Here is the good news about ending up with him. It brought me to the end of myself, which then landed me in therapy. THANK the universe, that I was referred to a fantastic therapeutic clinician, Kim Buehlman in Seattle, Washington. Kim knows that I am writing this and has okayed me sharing her name. Thanks, Kim! She had been trained in many techniques that she used on me immediately, two of which changed my life completely, and one we are using now. I will explain each of them to you in this book so you can try them on yourself, as well as point you to clinicians who are trained providers for each, in case you want to go deeper.

The first is called Lifespan Integration and the second is cognitive-behavioral therapy. Here my friends is the first key to getting the life that you want. Get your neurons connected and working properly!

"Where there is ruin, there is hope for a treasure." Rumi

What is Lifespan Integration, you ask? I'm telling you right now, it's sounds crazy and like magic or something, but it works!

Lifespan Integration (LI) is based on the notion that most of our emotional and thereby *life* dysfunction results from insufficient neural organization. Peggy Pace (2003), writes that due to trauma or neglect experienced during childhood, there may be a lack of connectivity between isolated neural networks which represent separate selves and self-states. This is why we think we are crazy and that a collection of misfits is running the show in our heads! Peggy goes on to say that psychological problems could also be caused by suboptimal integration between various regions and layers of the brain. That my friends, is the problem. The core problem. The reason you and I read self-help books, attend retreats, etc. and intently watch Gwyneth Paltrow on Netflix, learning how to breathe deeply, and still do not see long-lasting and permanent change in our lives. Our neurons will not allow it!

"Your task is not to seek for love, but merely to seek and find all the barriers within yourself that you have built against it."

—Rumi

So, in applying LI, the first thing that Kim had me do was to create a timeline of my life. This is what I want you to do as well. The timeline was to include memory cues from each year of my life going back as far as I could remember and up to present time. At the time, I was a hot mess (putting it mildly) and could not do it as "homework" in between sessions, so we did it together during our sessions. My first memory was swimming at the beach in Waikiki, Hawaii as a four-year-old and the present time memory is going shopping with my daughter, Maggie and looks something like this:

4 – swimming to rock wall at Waikiki

5 – running on grass at park

6 – seeing long grassy hill

7 – wearing uniforms at St. Patrick's

8 – playing war under the house with Michael and David

9 – watering trees in the backyard with Grandma Sally

10 – climbing the rope to the ceiling at school

11 – ambulance at house

12 – gymnastics camp in Kalispell

13 – cheerleading at football game in the rain

14 – roller skating with cousin Jerilyn

15 – the phone call – David

16 – Olympics in LA

17 – High School Graduation

18 - Etc etc (fill in for each year of life)

50 – climbing Mailbox Peak for my birthday

51 – going to Palma de Mallorca with David

52 – cutting down Christmas tree with Zoe and Maggie

Something recent – having lunch with parents

Something today – talking to Dominic

Open eyes and look around, you're here and back. Welcome back!

Once I had the timeline, we began Lifespan Integration. How it works is that, Kim would read my timeline and I would nod to her that I could see the memory cue in my mind's eye. Depending on what was happening with me at the moment (that is, my reason for being in therapy that day), we would start with the presenting problem and simply put we would go through the timelines. Now, depending on the situation at hand, I would come to find out there are different LI protocols. But, to keep it simple here, she would imaginally walk me through 2-3 repetitions or 8-9 repetitions and/or use an "affect bridge" to find a memory from my childhood, which had the similar feeling to the one I was experiencing that particular day. So, through the process of LI, the theory is that the self-system becomes increasingly more and better organized both in space and in time. Peggy Pace (2003) suggests that this increase in organization occurs in part due to the many shifts between selves and self-states which are required by repetitions of the LI Timeline. With repetitions of the Timeline, transitions between self-states become more fluid. This fluidity also contributes to the stability of the self-system. What I noticed as a patient and person is that I used to have a thought and get stuck in the thought, and I also thought that whatever

I was experiencing and thinking was true. LI understands this problem completely. Peggy's approach recognizes that what I was experiencing was a sense of being locked into a childhood time frame and being unaware that it was happening. Of course, the give-away looking back on it is that my reaction to life as an adult was not in proportion to the event. In other words, I would have a childlike or teenage-like response to an adult situation. Going back to the prostitute and free-time guy, I was not able to see him through an adult lens, I saw him through a child lens, which having now read something about my childhood, would make perfect sense to you. It made perfect sense to Kim then and does to me now.

So, after each LI session, I felt immediately calmer and able to see my current life stressor with more age appropriate eyes. I know that sounds weird, but it works. Lifespan Integration relies on the innate ability of the body-mind to heal itself. The difference between LI and other therapies is that LI is body-based, and combines active imagination, the juxtaposition of ego states in time, and a visual timeline of memories to facilitate neural integration and rapid healing. Other therapies are cognitive based only and therefore do not penetrate the body nor activate deeper memories, which unbeknownst (is that a word?) to us, are keeping us stuck.

During the integrating phase of LI, I was able to view each memory cue for each year of my life. The ideas is that LI causes memories to surface spontaneously, and because of how memories are held neurologically, each memory which surfaces is related to the emotional theme or issue being targeted. The resulting panoramic view of my life gave me new insights about lifelong patterns which resulted from the past trauma and allowed me to start feeling hope for the first time in my life. After some time, I finally realized that I was getting well.

As my mind started healing, I began being able to accept and love myself. I noticed that I started taking responsibility for my own life, because I started taking care of our own needs before involving myself with others, including my girls, friends, family, and work. Up until this point, I had what you read, lack of differentiation, multigenerational emotional processes, porous boundaries, and on and on. I was not able to get any traction with making lasting change in my life either. Now, seemingly like magic, I am avoiding situations that put me at risk physically, morally, psychologically or spiritually. I started becoming the person I wanted to be and became honest in expressing who I was, developing true intimacy in my relationships with myself and with others. Amazing!

The next therapeutic technique she used was cognitive behavioral therapy (CBT). In conjunction with LI, CBT worked for me because it focuses on challenging and changing unhelpful cognitive distortions and behaviors. As a result of this focus, I was able to improve my emotional regulation, and develop personal coping strategies as well as target and resolve current problems. CBT utilizes several techniques, which I will not go into. Instead I want to introduce you to the intervention that worked. Kim introduced me to "The Work" of Byron Katie. Now this will probably sound crazy too, I know. You must bear with me and try it before you scoff completely and toss the book in the corner, because it works. Okay?

Byron Katie (BK) calls "The Work" a meditative practice. OMG, I know I've lost you now! Hold on! So, she suggests simply that you notice who or what is upsetting you, angering you, or saddening you. Once you have that, you write down why and what the specific situation is. Second, she suggests that you write all the stressful thoughts down, using short and simple sentences. Third, we start to question the thoughts one at a time and allow our most authentic selves to answer. Next, we look for what she calls a "turnaround." The turnaround is the opposite of the initial stressful thought. Finally, we look at the turn around and consider whether it is also true or truer than the original thought. Let me give you an example from my life back in the day. This thought makes me laugh now but used to plague me 10-years ago.

<u>Initial Thought</u>: He shouldn't be friends with so many girls on Facebook.

<u>Is it true</u>: Yes.

<u>Can I absolutely know that it is true</u>: Yes.

<u>How do I feel, what do I think, how do I behave when I think this thought</u>: Like a complete loser and jerk. I need to leave this guy, but am stuck. I feel hopeless. I don't think he'll ever change. My life sucks and is not getting better. This is a disaster in the making. I am so screwed. There is no way out. I should change my name and move to Canada.

<u>Who would I be if I couldn't have this thought</u>: Wow, I would just move on with my day, I guess. I would be fine. I'd be my wonderful, funny, adorable self. Geez. That's a nice thought.

<u>Turnaround #1</u>: I shouldn't be friends with so many girls on Facebook.

<u>Three ways in which this thought is true or truer</u>: #1 – Facebook takes a lot of time and I might be better off without it, #2 – What does gender have to do with anything? Nothing, #3 – They aren't really "friends," (although some are) they're just connections.

<u>Turnaround #2</u>: He should be friends with so many girls on Facebook.

<u>Three ways in which this thought is true or truer</u>: #1 – He seems to really like social media. It brings him joy, #2 – It's happening, #3 – Again, they aren't really "friends," it's just what Facebook calls a connection.

Turnaround #3: I should be friends with so many girls on Facebook.

<u>Three ways in which this thought is true or truer</u>: #1 – Being

connected to people is probably good for me, #2 – Being friends with girls is also probably good for me, #3 – It's happening.

So, by the time I get to the third turnaround, inevitably I'm feeling 1,000 percent better and I can see that even though the initial thought is true, so are the turn arounds. This helps my mind, which was initially stuck (and as a result, angry) to loosen up and move on. Once my mind moves on, so does my body, and my life. Yay!

This is what worked for me. I would come into Kim's office and have a presenting problem of some sort and she would walk me through LI and then a few BK worksheets, and I would leave feeling like I had some options for my life. Now, keep in mind that this took a while. By a while, I will be honest and say several years. Part of the length of time was that I worked full time and was a single mother, so only saw Kim about once a month. You could certainly go faster, and I would recommend doing this work daily and on yourself, if that is your goal. That's what I do. I have worked Kim out of a job, which by-the-way, she is fine with. I will put additional resources and worksheets in the final chapter of this book for you to follow.

One last comment about these suggestions. Keep in mind that starting to use them will feel awkward. I am a mediocre tennis player and decided I wanted to get better, so look lessons. The first thing my tennis coach did was teach me a new grip for holding my racket. It was super hard to get used to. I couldn't keep it up for long and resorted back to my old grip over and over. We stayed with it and now I use my new grip more often than the old one. These new techniques will feel the same. You'll struggle to do a CBT on yourself or walk through Lifespan Integration, even though your mind is pestering you with a thought that you know isn't true. You won't think it will work, so won't try it. I get that. Do it anyway. I always tell the people that I work with that you can't wait to "feel like it" or to be ready. Ready isn't one of the steps in any of these ideas. It works only if you work it, so give yourself a break from your mind, and give it a go. See you in the next chapter!

Chapter 4

One Final Suggestion:
What's Happening Now

"When I stopped living in the problem and started living in the solution, the problem went away"

The Big Book of Alcoholics Anonymous (p. 417)

Today, I still see Kim and we still do Lifespan Integration and Byron Katie CBT-type worksheets, which finally allowed me to not just handle life's stressors, but to thrive under whatever life presents, with detachment and presence. Remember that "letting go" skill we discussed in an earlier chapter. Now, when something happens, I don't find myself needing to let go, because the truth is that I don't attach in the first place.

I remember years ago, prior to dating the guy we discussed (so I couldn't blame him), I had just finished my doctorate, had a great job, that paid well, was interesting and professionally challenging, and yet was completely miserable. I had read lots of self-help books and been to therapy, but only the talk-type. I had not yet done any trauma or CBT work, so I would find myself regularly on the floor of my bathroom, distraught and crying. I really had no skills for living. Looking back on it, I realize that in addition to being traumatized, I had never been taught things like boundaries, self-care, self-love, work-life balance, personal values, healthy body image, and on and on. These remained conceptual until I was introduced to the deeper work, which rewired my mind, and taught me how to embody each idea, into my life specifically (not life in general). That is the trick my friends!

Case in point, I started dating again. One of the first dates was with my former Pilates instructor. We used to chat briefly after class sometimes, so I got to know him over a few months period. I thought he was pretty cute, he certainly had an incredible body, and seemed well read, so when he said we should grab a tea sometime, I thought "sure!" This guy always had a book with him, was happy to talk philosophy, and was a Pilates instructor for goodness sake, so he must be well. We had a great time at tea. Fantastic, in fact. He was smart, attractive, and had a good stable job. All important partner qualities in my estimation. Afterward, I consulted with my crew of girlfriends and Laura (one of them) said to me, "it's amazing that he owns his own home as a Pilates instructor. It's so expensive here. I wonder how he did that?" Humm, great point dear friend, Laura, I wondered too. Now, I have by this time been through significant amounts of Lifespan Integration and CBT, as well as am an active member of a 12-step program, so have learned one or two things in my tenure on this more healthy side of life. One important behavior that I embody now is, I wait for people to reveal who they are, before I go all in. Actually, what is more true, is that I don't go all in anymore. I don't leave myself for people or situations. What this looks like is I no longer go along to get along, I don't get swept off my feet, I let you be who you are and I'll stay over here being who I am. We can meet in the middle. At least I will meet you in the middle and if you are not able to go there, then that's fine too. Take care.

Okay, back to Pilates guy. He reached out again to see if I wanted to have lunch. I was super happy about that and said, "yes!" As we were having our amazing lunch, I remembered Laura's question and so asked. "Hey, it's so great that you are a homeowner in this expensive market, especially as a Pilates instructor. How'd you pull that off?" He said, "oh thanks, I am able to afford my place because I used to have a roommate, but then my girlfriend moved in, so we share the expenses." I was all, "gosh, look at the time, gotta go!" I never saw him again. I didn't need to work it out with him, or figure it out. Having a girlfriend was a deal-breaker, not a work around for me. Prior to blocking him on my phone, I sent him a text and let him know that, "I didn't date men who were in a committed relationship, and that I would not be seeing him again." He was baffled by my response, by the way, and said, "Laura, I didn't mean anything by it. Why can't we still see each other?" "Wow, really?" I wrote, "Well, I did mean something. Don't contact me again."

So here we are. I did all the work and now have the skills, I so desperately wanted years ago. It feels like magic at times. I look at myself and am so ridiculously grateful and amazed that I FINALLY have the life that I wanted all along. I have two beautiful, well-adjusted and happy daughters, a robust and impactful career, a pile of amazing friends that I adore, a close relationship with my parents, and life-enriching hobbies. More than all of that, on the inside I feel calm, confident, and well. I have a quiet mind. It doesn't pester me anymore. If a stressful thought arises, I'm happy about it now, because it's so rare. All stressful thoughts, emotions, and behaviors get put through the processes outlined in this book and I don't let them go, they let me go. As a result, I have some power to positively affect my life and regularly advocate for what I want. I have also become less loyal. I don't keep people, organizations, or situations in my life that do not align with my values. Upon awakening, I used to be griped with fear, and now my eyes open and I look forward to my day and forward to experiencing what happens. It's all good.

"People are disconnected from themselves and therefore each other"

Eckhart Tolle "Power of Now" (p. 9)

Kim has me now doing what is called Complex Integration of Multiple Brain Systems (CIMBS) work. Okay friends, this is the final piece of the puzzle, and may sound the craziest! But it works! On top of everything else, it turns out that my brain was (at times) suppressing feelings, which kept me in avoidance. So weird, I know. You gotta try this one too, because it's super awkward! Basically, CIMBS, "uses targeted therapeutic interventions to modulate the suppression, differentiation and/or activation of the different Brain Systems that have been wired together in a person's brain by early developmental experiences or traumas," (http:// www.complexintegrationmbs.com/).

What this looks like in session, is that I sit with my eyes open and experience myself. Kim looks at me and I look at her. It's odd, believe me. She'll say things like, "we're here to be with you." "Tell me how you are feeling right now?" "Great!" "Where do you feel that in your body?" "Great! Let's stay with that." This goes on for 20-30 minutes. I gotta tell you folks that crazy as it sounds, it actually makes me feel great! I leave every session feeling like I have options in my life, can advocate for my wants, can take care of myself, can do nothing too. It's fantastic!

> **"Without grounding we are unstable. We lose our center, fly off the handle, get swept off our feet, or daydream in the fantasy world. We lose our ability to contain, which is the ability to have and to hold. If we cannot contain, we cannot hold our boundaries and build up inner power; thus, we cannot mature"**
>
> **Anodea Judith "Eastern Body Western Mind" (p. 63)**

Basically, what she is doing is supporting me to notice and reinforce positive feelings, which then strengthens new adaptive neuropathways. It also moves my internal experience from avoiding how I am feeling to actually feeling how I am feeling. It's all about learning to be in the moment, which ALL the self-help books tell us is the key to happiness. I finally got it AND more importantly know how to keep it.

One of the gifts of this work has been the authenticity of my relationships. I shared briefly about my father. He and I didn't speak for 30-years, until one day, about a year into doing LI and BK, I decided to change that and called him. Turns out he had gotten sober. He and I become fast friends, talking frequently, sharing a quick wit, love of true crime, and fondness for the Geico gecko. Who knew? He passed away two-years-ago, and I was able to be by his side and hold his hand. He held mine too. We no longer needed anything from each other and felt only gratitude and love.

The other relationship that I value today is that with my mother. She is such an incredible lady, about which another book could be written. She pulled herself from an abusive childhood home and vowed she would never hit her children and she never did. She put herself through college, raised three kids on her own, and gave us her all. I have so much love and respect for her. A lady of substance, she is!

Then there are my girls. Truth be told, and my friends know this well, I was full of resentment toward them before I did this work. All I could see was how much they needed and how little I had to give. As I have learned, I got it right but backward. I had a lot to give and they needed so little. They have allowed me change, for the better. I used to think that David was my soul, but now it belongs (at least in part) to my girls, Zoe and Maggie. They are both A students, extremely funny, and truly themselves. What a gift!

The last relationship that I truly admire is the one I have with my higher power. Some call it God, or higher self, or universal energy. Whatever it is, I am grateful. All I know is that I have no interest in doing this life thing on my own, even with a quiet and healed mind. Upon awakening every morning, I roll on my knees and pray. I then move to meditation, journaling, and read soul-enriching literature for about an hour. I have learned that grounding myself before the day gets going keeps me balanced, centered, calm, and well.

All of this work created within me the ability to connect those seemingly disconnected concepts from chapter 1. No more crying on the bathroom floor. Now that my mind is healed, I can attend to schema acquisition for all those seemingly bewildering concepts that require high element interactivity and therefore higher cognitive load. Thank you dissertation! The projector has been fixed. In the next chapter, it's your turn. Go get your life!

Chapter 5

Your Turn

Below I have provided links to each technique mentioned in this book. Please click around each one to find answers to any questions that you might have. There also are skilled providers for each, that would be happy to walk you through the techniques personally. Remember that it only works if you work it, so go for it!

Lifespan Integration https://lifespanintegration.com/

Create your Timeline: Remember for this, you need to find a memory cue for each year of your life, going back to your earliest memory and ending with something that happened today. You can fill it in here and/or get a blank piece of paper and start there.

Earliest memory:

4

5

6

7

8

9

10

11

12

13

14

15

16

17

18

19

20

21

22

23

24

25

26

27

28

29

30

31

32

33

34

35

36

37

38

39

40

41

42

43

44

Something recent –

Something today –

Open eyes and look around, you're here and back. Welcome back!

Cognitive behavioral therapy (CBT)

Remember in the book that I mentioned that CBT worked for me because it focuses on challenging and changing unhelpful cognitive distortions and behaviors. You read some of my story, so know that I had plenty of opportunity to see the world (and my life) from a distorted lens. As a result of CBT, I was able to gain new focus, improve my emotional regulation, and develop personal coping strategies as well as target and resolve current problems. The CBT approach I am introducing you to was created by Byron Katie (BK) and is called, "The Work." BK offers all of her worksheets for free at her website https://thework.com/, so there is no need to reproduce them here. Let me just give you a few of her prompts to get you going. There are also countless certified and skilled practitioners who use and teach "The Work," so please try them out if you need.

Initial Thought:

Is it true:

Can I absolutely know that it is true:

How do I feel, what do I think, how do I behave when I think this thought:

<u>Who would I be if I couldn't have this thought</u>:

<u>Turnaround #1</u>:

<u>Three ways in which this thought is true or truer</u>

<u>Turnaround #2</u>:

<u>Three ways in which this thought is true or truer</u>:

<u>Turnaround #3</u>:

<u>Three ways in which this thought is true or truer</u>

Complex Integration of Multiple Brain Systems (CIMBS)

Okay friends, this is the final piece of the puzzle, and may sound the craziest! But it works! Here is the website to find more information and to find practitioners in the field, http://www. complexintegrationmbs.com/.

In addition to LI and CBT, I use CIMBS on myself daily is to look for warmth, positive, or happy feelings in my body. Once I locate one of these, I spend time expanding them to the rest of my body and sit with it for a few minutes. CIMBS works because it increases my brain capability through creating differentiation as well as increased neural integration and flexibility. Through repetition (I do it everyday), I reinforce the strength of "positive" and "well" neural networks, which then perpetuate positivity, which becomes become faster and more automatic. It leaves me with a sense of balance.

Here is what you would do:

- Sit with your eyes open and experience yourself.

- Scan your body to see how you are actually feeling.

- If you don't feel anything, wait until you do.

- Find a positive feeling in your body. Something will arise.

- Note the positive feeling and where it is located.

- Expand the feeling throughout the body.

- Sit for 10-15 minutes and experience the feeling in your body.

That's it! Keep practicing these techniques until they become your practice and by all means, live your best life. You got this!

In deepest healing, Laura

A Note to Writers of Self-Help Books

As you have read, the literature is clear in its suggestion that people process information differently. The literature discloses that delivery and design practices for any type of instruction, have traditionally been determined by common sense, not cognitive or learning theory. This is largely true because until recently, neither cognitive science nor educational theory have generated sufficient findings to permit extensive application to either consideration (Sweller, 1990).

Based on my experiences, research on trauma, and findings stated above, authors of self-help books, retreat organizers, instructional designers, and trainers must consider the ideas pointed out in this book and employ strategies that reduce or eliminate the need for the people to use cognitive resources and therefore limit their ability to attend to schema acquisition. Where instruction focuses on behavioral change, as is typically the case with self-help material, this is perhaps even more critical. It is noted that instead of lecturing to students about the theory of behavioral change in the workplace, materials should be created (specifically, quick reference guides, worked sample, and illustrations) that allow for schema acquisition, thereby increasing self-awareness and therefore creating the needed behavioral change people want.

Additional Resources

Pia Mellody

Facing Codependence: What It Is, Where It Comes from, How It Sabotages Our Lives

Facing Love Addiction: Giving Yourself the Power to Change the Way You Love

Jalal al-Din Rumi

The Essential Rumi

Emmet Fox

Sermon on the Mount

Bill Wilson and Dr. Bob Smith

The Big Book of Alcoholics Anonymous

Eckhart Tolle

The Power of Now

Terry Real

The New Rules of Marriage: What You Need to Know to Make Love Work

Byron Katie

Loving What Is: Four Questions That Can Change Your Life

A Mind at Home with Itself: How Asking Four Questions Can Free Your Mind, Open Your Heart, and Turn Your World Around

I Need Your Love, Is That True?: How to Stop Seeking Love, Approval, and Appreciation and Start Finding Them Instead

A Thousand Names for Joy: Living in Harmony with the Way Things Are

Bill P, Todd W, et al.

Drop the Rock: Removing Character Defects - Steps Six and Seven

Dr. Helen Schucman

A Course in Miracles

Anne Lamott

Hallelujah Anyway: Rediscovering Mercy

Anodea Judith, Laura Jennings, et al.

Eastern Body, Western Mind: Psychology and the Chakra System as a Path to the Self

Kahlil Gibran

The Prophet

Dr. John N. Briere and Catherine Scott

Principles of Trauma Therapy: A Guide to Symptoms, Evaluation, and Treatment (DSM-5 Update)

Patricia C. Broderick and Pamela Blewitt

The Life Span: Human Development for Helping Professionals

Geri Miller

Learning the Language of Addiction Counseling

Richard S. Sharf

Theories of Psychotherapy & Counseling: Concepts and Cases

12-Step Community Resources

Alcoholics Anonymous https://aa.org/

Codependents Anonymous https://coda.org/

Al-Anon Family Groups https://al-anon.org/

Sex and Love Addicts Anonymous https://slaafws.org/

Adult Children of Alcoholics https://adultchildren.org/

Therapeutic Technique Resources

Lifespan Integration Resources

https://lifespanintegration.com/

Byron Katie International

https://thework.com

Complex Integration of Multiple Brain Systems

http://www.complexintegrationmbs.com

Quick Reference Guide

Section One: The Reason Self-Help Books Don't Work (Chapter 1 and 2)

Childhood Trauma

Cognitive Theory of Multimedia Learning

Dual-Coding Theory

Schema Acquisition

Cognitive Load Theory

Linear vs Non-Linear Thinking

Lifeworld

Cultural Trauma

Societal Trauma

Differentiation of Self

Multigenerational Emotional Processing

Section Two: How to Get them to Work! (Chapter 3, 4, and 5)

Lifespan Integration

https://lifespanintegration.com/

Byron Katie "The Work"

https://thework.com

Complex Integration of Multiple Brain Systems

http://www.complexintegrationmbs.com

References

Habermas, J. (1981). *The theory of communicative action: Reason and the rationalization of society*, Vol. 1. (T. McCarthy, Trans.). Boston: Beacon Press.

Anderson, R. C. (1973). Learning principles from text. *Journal of Educational Psychology, 64* (1), 26–30.

Clark, R. E. (Ed.). (2001). *Learning from media: Arguments, analysis, and evidence.* Greenwich, CT: Information Age Publishing.

Clark, J. M., Paivio, A. (1991). Dual coding theory and education. *Educational Psychology Review, 3*(3), 149–210.

Mayer, R. E. (1996). Learning strategies for making sense out of expository text: The SOI model for guiding three cognitive processes in knowledge construction. *Educational Psychology Review, 8*, 357–371.

Mayer, R. E. (1997). Multimedia learning: Are we asking the right questions? *Educational Psychologist, 32*, 1–19.

Mayer, R. E. (2001). *Multimedia learning.* Cambridge, UK: Cambridge University Press.

Mayer, R. E., Sims, V. K. (1994). For whom is a picture worth a thousand words? Extensions of dual-coding theory of multimedia learning. *Journal of Educational Psychology, 86*(3), 389–401.

Nichols, M. P. (2013). *Family therapy: Concepts and methods.* Boston: Pearson.

Pace, P. (2003). *Lifespan Integration Connecting Ego States Through Time.* US: Eirene Imprint.

Paivio, A. (1986). *Mental representations: A dual coding approach.* Oxford, England: Oxford University Press.

Paivio, A. (1991). Dual coding theory: Retrospect and current status. *Canadian Journal of Psychology Outstanding Contributions Series, 45*(3), 255–287.

Sadoski, M., Paivio, A. (2001). *Imagery and text: A dual coding theory of reading and writing.* Mahwah, NJ: Lawrence Erlbaum Associates, Publishers.

Sweller, J., Chandler, P., Tierney, P. & Cooper, M. (1990).

Cognitive load as a factor in the structuring of technical material. *Journal of Experimental Psychology, 119*(2), 176–192.

Sweller, J., Chandler, P. (1991). Evidence for cognitive load theory. *Cognition and Instruction, 8*(4), 351–362.

Sweller, J., Chandler, P. (1994). Why some material is difficult to learn. *Cognition and instruction, 12*(3), 185–233.

Williamson, L. (2004). *The Effects of Instructional Strategies on the Learning of Procedures for Production Employees in a High-Technology Manufacturing Environment.* (unpublished doctoral dissertation). Nova Southeastern University.

Acknowledgements

I want to thank Kim Buehlman. Kim, you have steered me so competently and calmly over the years. When you pushed, it was always with deep affection. I understand today that it was attunement. It was because of our deep therapeutic work that I wanted to add to my professional toolbelt the strategies, theories, and tools covered in this book in order to help others on a deeper level, hopefully showing them the way, as you did for me. Thank you. I will pay it forward, Kim.

I am also deeply indebted to my close friends and confidants, especially Laura Bridenback and Tarsi Hall. These two ladies have stood with me shoulder to shoulder through much of what was written. I have so much love and admiration for you both and thank you from the bottom of my heart.

Because of all of this work, I am truly surrounded by an incredible set of friends and colleagues, whom I would also like to thank for their insights into this work including Alicia Pucci, David Griffin, David Schwartz, Kurt Kirstein, Liz Fountain,

Meg Trainer Reade, Karen Langer, Dominic Zambito, Orla Concannon, Payam Saadat, Tammie Starwich, Britt Eckhart, Jodey Farwell, Cherry Leung, Tom Cary, Sophie Haccou, Monika Petrova, Autumn Nelson, Carolyn Galloway, Charlie Manger, Cory Viehl, Joyce Mphande-Finn, Susan LaDonna, Libbie Stellas, and Walt Channell.

Finally, I would like to thank my family. My parents, Lisa Murphy-Perin, Gordon Perin, and Steve and Debbie Williamson are and were each extraordinary people. As you read in my story, they struggled with their own issues, but they also gave completely of themselves to the best of their abilities to each other and our family. My Aunt, Lisa Sandoval significantly supported me over the years as well. Her straight-talking no-nonsense approach always pointed me in the right direction, whether I liked it or not!

Zoe and Maggie Popovich, my two-daughters, must also be acknowledged. I am grateful beyond measure for these two, their curiosity and quick wit as well as the depth of their hearts, stand out. They never let me off the hook and have taught me the true meaning of the word, "love." The universe shined on me the day they were born. May I continue to grow into the mother that you deserve. I love you!

Finally, my clients have given me so much, but one in particular stands out, J. I'm not allowed to share your name, but you know who you are. Thank you for reminding me that every day is a 30-day party!

About the Author

Dr. Laura Williamson is truly passionate about supporting people at any stage and ability, to transform their lives. As a researcher, writer, therapist, and educator, with over 20 articles, book chapters, instructional CD's, and professional presentations in publication, she views the process of learning and psychological development through a trauma-informed, family systems, and cognitive-behavioral therapy lens, each of which have been influenced by her extensive training and experience. Several notable influences include LifeSpan Integration, "The Work" by Byron Katie, Cognitive Load Theory, Schema Acquisition Theory, and Relational Life Therapy.

She is also dedicated to organizational transformation. Recognizing the need for today's organizations to fully integrate knowledge about trauma into their policies, procedures, and practices, she is passionate about creating business solutions as they present at the intersection of data- and relational-centered systems.

This is no small task and she loves the challenge! Two examples of finding these solutions follow. In an effort to create accessibility for those who would not otherwise pursue a higher education, she created a roadmap for learning and outreach with Seattle area chambers to develop stackable and portable business microcredits around specific study areas, such as finance, HR, accounting, and more. These areas now align with the following professional certifications CPA, CMA, CFA, PCM, CAPM, PMP, SHRM-CP, SHRM-SCP, CAP, which are globally recognized and portable and able to reach a diverse student market. For the second example, she established and implemented success metrics for stakeholders internal to the organization and worked with the system to deploy them at scale, revising on a continual basis based on feedback and data. She insisted on the highest standards through creating metrics around instructional, curriculum, and delivery performance, which are now being rolled out to the entire university, resulting in improvement in faculty performance in exceeding standards from 13% to 83%.

Additionally, Laura holds five degrees starting with a BA in Philosophy, MBA in Leadership, EdD in Instructional Technology, MEd in Adult Education for Diverse Learners, and MA in Counseling. Her therapeutic work has been with the YWCA Angeline's Day Center, WA State Women's Correctional Facility, PEER Seattle, and the CityU of Seattle Counseling Center where she engaged in individual, couples, and group therapy focusing on addiction, grief and loss, stress management, assertive communication, cognitive distortions and relapse prevention. Her industry experience includes private sector work with several west coast firms including Data I/O Corporation, Boeing Computer Services, Physio-Control, and L-3 Corporation, where she was responsible for a variety of educational technology, technical training, and process improvement projects including the development and delivery of technical manuals, trainings and programs (using multimedia methodologies) such as interactive CD-ROMs, job-aids, reports, and quick reference guides with clients such as the LAPD, the US Coast Guard, and KTLA News in Los Angeles California to name a few.

Finally, she has worked for over twenty-five years in higher education in the capacity of adjunct faculty, dissertation chair, dissertation committee member, professor, program director, and associate dean. For four universities she has designed and taught courses for online delivery, international, hybrid, ESL, and face-to-face formats using WebCT, eCollege, and Blackboard platforms.

Printed in the United States
By Bookmasters

Printed in the United States
By Bookmasters